Lucky Men; Unluckily Me

A collection of poems

Mathias I. Brookes

Table of Contents

Dedication

This is dedicated to my mom, no matter how many times we fought, you always believed in me. Even beyond the living veil you keep watching out for me.

About the Author

Mathias has spent her whole life being silent. She spent her childhood years being bounced around in the foster care system. One constant thing is and always will be literature, while that's reading or writing. After the loss of her mom in 2023 she decided it was time to start doing more than writing and saving her journals. She decided it was time to speak up not only for her but her family.

Appreciation

I want to start this off differently than how most things should start!

I want to start by saying thank you to none other than you the reader!

Even if you read the first poem and decide this is not for me thank you for even picking this up!

We say don't judge a book by its cover but we all know that's never the case! It's more don't judge and create preconceived things in your head; because we all know we Look at the cover and go "This looks good" but put it back for being cookie cutter sweetness when we want raw and unfiltered reality.

So Again Thank You!

I'm not going to say I hope you enjoy but I do hope that the words in this book make a difference in your life and those around you!

Time to Stand

To all the men who have used my body before in any way.

This is not for you.

This is for all the times you made me feel incompetent, less than, not even human.

This is for all those times. I wanted to scream but never wanted to let anyone hear.

This is for the times that I knew I would die if I did not comply.

I know I keep saying what this is for. But honestly, if you're reading this;

This is for you.

Because I spoke up, so you didn't have to.

I decided to let the world in on who's been within me.

And I think I'm good with that.

Especially with what the United States has come to, Now that we no longer have control of our bodies.

I think that once my children come of age and hear of this story, They will be proud to call me their mother.

Not only will she say that her mom survived.

She will say, "My mom lived.

And she told her story.

My mom did the things.

Only women dream of because they could never tell their side without seeming like a VICTIM or the BLAMER,"

or the LIAR.

Many people think that this is going to be easy.

I'm here to tell you.

With every page and sentence, and even

EVERY SINGLE

word written.

I cried tears flowing down my face like the river flowing in the Nile.

It's not because I don't want to share these stories but it's because with almost every story in here, there is a small price to pay and I wasn't ready to pay any of it.

I learned to take it day by day and that's how the tears stopped taking such a toll.

I learned how to live with it.

Mathias I. Brookes

He Him Mister

He told me "I was beautiful".

He told me I was mature.

He said I was Brave even though I knew I was a coward.

He got close to me.

So close that no matter what way I moved a part of me was
touching him.

He Him Mister

He pulled my pants down.

Pulled my shirt up; and used it to make me not be able to make a
sound.

I tried to run but I was frozen.

in my mind I'm thinking, hoping, wishing he stops.

that one thing you think is never going to happen to you and now
it's happening to ME

He Him Mister

He used my Scarf to tie my hands together.

I already could not move and now I am paralyzed.

Why me? Why does it have to be me?

I beg and plead and just cry.

He says it's my fault because I wore what I wore around him and the way I looked at him.

I WANTED IT;

I wanted HIM

He Him Mister

He forced himself into me,

Fourteen-year-old Me.

He took it away and it hurts so bad.

He kept kissing me.

There was blood everywhere and he then flipped me over.

I'm not even sure what he's going to do when he gets done.

My sadness has turned into rage.

He Him Mister

Flood Gates Open

I shouldn't have let this happen.

I should have been stronger.

As he gets off and pull his pants all the way down,

I kick him and i do all i could.

I run and run and run.

HE HIM MISTER

Mathias I. Brookes

Family Man

Now this guy.

He is someone Familiar.

He is someone we all know.

No, not this particular person, you don't know him by his first
name because he is no one to you

YET,

but me.

He is the one who started this ALL.

I don't blame the last man, anymore.

Because this man

NO DARE I SAY THIS BOY

Made it to where I was never able to gain that innocence back.

At night, You would come into my room

and you would tell me, *"Remember when you were little, we used to play this game."*

"You know I'd never do anything to hurt you."

"You know, I love you"

"You know, you're special."

WELL FUCK YOU.

I no longer feel special anymore.

I no longer feel like you love me,

If you do, I don't want it anymore.

God, Your love is *disgusting and intoxicating*

The same **LOVE** that says we are supposed to be family!

I now know I looked at things through colored lenses.

What **YOU** did is called **RAPE**!

I can't remember the so-called "game" we played but I now know that it wasn't right whatever it was.

I wanted to kill you but instead, I took your power away!

Your lies will never know the inside of my head anymore because I now know.

I blocked you out and made sure there was no way in.

You're a monster.

Mathias I. Brookes

The Nice Guy

Gosh, I don't know where to start.

You,

My God,

You

I guess it's time to open this *jar* I tucked away in my heart

Those *soft, kind* eyes.

I'd get lost every time we spoke.

You showed me love.

That kind of love that makes you have butterflies.

The kind of love that everyone goes *"Awe aren't they so cute."*

Your love made me have a love for my body.

When I thought it was not for me.

You showed me, Kindness.

The kind of kindness I thought only came with pity, but there was never any pity in your eyes.

When I wanted to end it all,

You made me believe we could go against the world.

It was so great I thought I was on a High.

The Kissing, touching.

My God

Dare I say it; The Sex.

All good things come to an End; Right?

I just wish the end wasn't so close for us.

As you made me feel like I needed to feel.

You gave me a warm embrace.

Thank You.

Where part of me thought I didn't deserve it.

I started to self-sabotage because why would a guy like you ever truly want to be with a broken girl like me?

You are one of the good guys in my story.

While you are a Good Guy I think you came at the wrong time.

When things went south for us I began to crave something I had only wished was a *mirage*.

This!!

This very moment is where my drug began.

So, while our time was short it was very memorable.

So thank you, Mister Nice Guy.

Older Guy

You.

You were there on the back of the bus.

You were my dare I say

First. Victim.

This is:

Once I realized I had a problem.

I lied to you big time on the back of that bus.

"How old are you?" you asked with that honey-smooth voice

"17!" I fired back maybe a bit too fast

I can say with certainty I'm happy It was you.

No one else would have probably been able to help me.

Feel like you made me feel.

At that time!

Not the way that you did.

I do believe, however,

If it was someone else I would be a fucked up person because

You showed me; It really can be enjoyed.

You showed me that it could be emotionless.

You showed me that It can be Fun.

You also showed me; It can be Fucking Crazy.

But you didn't show me and didn't tell me that it can hurt.

Once it goes away,

it makes you feel like you are in a bottomless pit.

And also, only ever momentary

Which SUCKS.

Because that's what made me want it more.

You are the reason I discovered the power the female body truly
has over the male mind.

Over the male body as a whole.

I'd Say thank you but I don't think my other victims would like
that.

Project Rat Care

I don't mean to sound like an asshole.

But sadly to the next few: you guys are not important!

In this aspect, you add nothing to my story other than the occasional fun tidbits.

Maybe one day I'll share everyone met in this part of my life.

You are however important in my journey because you guys were my rats if you will.

You helped me perfect my state of mind over matter.

You helped me know exactly how much I could push the male mind to get what I wanted.

Now mind you I did fall for some of you guys but not like *him* or ***HIM.***

I fell for you like you would fall for your favorite person in that book you love; the one who always dies.

You guys never made it in me per se but you did help others who came after and for that I feel I should at least mention that I used you. For that, I am sorry and hope you are now Happy.

Not that it would matter because you never knew I used you i made sure you felt you were getting something out of it!

Now I kinda feel bad when I can't sleep and I think back on the things I regret; some of you come to mind.

I remember driving one of you so far that you thought you could get my attention being broken; I can never say sorry enough.

Married Man

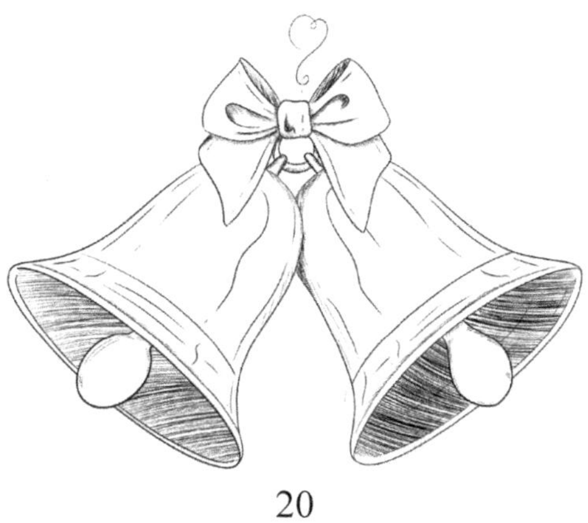

20

That number is the number of years between Mister Hero and I.

Gosh Thanks to those rats, I was able to get all I wanted from you.

You kinda became my first sugar daddy, didn't you?

Not only was it great but you were huge.

I was practically a rag doll in your arms.

Now I know you're thinking, if it was so great why is this man in the story?

Well, He was *36*.

I can write this now and not get anyone in trouble.

Had I known what I do now I would have never said *"hi"*.

You are Fucking Married!

Luckily, I didn't want to ruin things.

I would have told someone about you!

You could tell I started to hate you.

"We aren't happy, Sweets!"

"We are only in it for the kids. We don't want them to not see us in the same house."

Things you said and I believed it because I wanted the EUPHORIA that came along with you had me blindsided.

What's worse you weren't alone in getting me to fall for your charm.

You had, dare I say an accomplice.

She made it sound like it was okay to do what I was doing.

And for that I also Hate her! She was supposed to be my Family.

What's worse is later when I told a friend she told me you both belong in jail and sometimes; I wish I did tell.

Just know it was never for you but for your kids to not be without you.

On that note, I'm done talking about You.

JV Football Player

Holy shit I almost forgot about you!

Mister football player

I was in 10th Grade and you were in 9th.

My mom had fucked up when I met you.

She made us move to your side of town.

She and my stepfather were arguing, we moved to make her comfortable.

You were kind.

You were a great listener.

Hell almost made me want to stop using men.

Then you ruined it.

You started to make everything sexual while in age you were less than you accounted for everything else.

You got into my head; and made me cry on your shoulder.

Tears rushing down my face you fucking kissed me.

What happened next I want to blame you but it was of my own volition.

Like something inside me had turned on; something I tried so hard to push down.

But like vomit it always gets its way.

I led you inside and you followed because you were confused.

I told you I was home alone. I took that kiss and ran with it.

I told you I just wanted to talk inside not once did you tell me no.

Hell, all signs pointed to yes.

I fucked you! I could tell you didn't know what the fuck you were doing.

It ended and I said to get out.

You asked, "WHY?" "Did I do something wrong?"

I ignored you the next day at the bus stop.

You caved and grabbed me at school.

"Talk to me! You take my virginity and then ignore me. Who the fuck does that?"

I said sorry I can't do this. Let's talk after school on the bus.

I missed the bus on purpose that day.

You got the hint. I Am Very Sorry!

In my head, I became the monster that day.

And I needed to stay far away from good people.

Like YOU

You were the one who let me get to know an old addiction.

Self Harming.

Mister Has Been

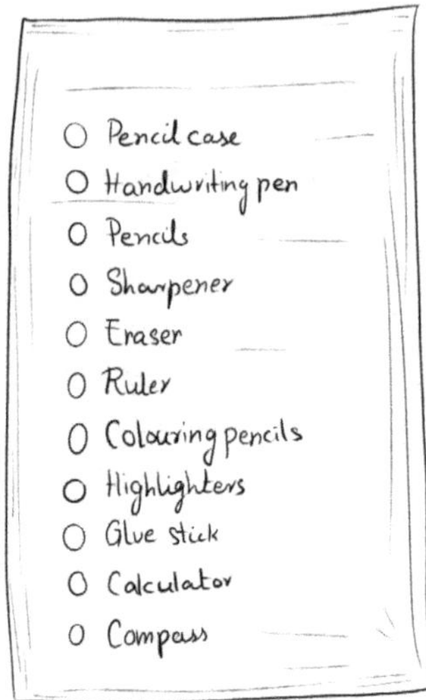

Oh my Mister Used To be one of the top five hot guys.

I wish I didn't have a lot to say about you.

You are exactly what I wanted after fucking up.

You are a Tall glass of tiny dick energy.

What Does that mean; you ask.

It means the asshole had a shred of decency to realize he couldn't use me the way he wanted.

I mean Obviously, we had sex.

Funny story You could never make me cum! But I used you to find my next victim.

He came to me because you talked to your boys about everything!

I knew he would come and COME running.

He's wanted me since middle school back when I had no breasts.

What I didn't know was that you would be so bitter!

I had to make it known that we had played around so that he knew
I didn't give a fuck about you.

Once, some people found out that's where a tiny bit of my
problems started.

Sorry Sweet girl, I didn't know you guys were together and I'm so
sorry he said you were not his type.

I mean I get it. You were an asshole.

What I don't get is that he still dumped you once you found out.

He came after me and I had already set my eyes on someone else.

Which Dare I say made the hunt even better, more fun.

Funny Twin

Hello there Mister twin

Yes, it is your turn.

The funny thing is I enjoyed our time.

You were Fun.

You wanted to spend quality time together.

I honestly didn't see you coming!

Did I change my mind about using you?

HELL NO

You made it all too easy. Not only did you come running, I had you wrapped around my finger.

All I had to do was say one little word.

You were practically begging after that.

How could your friend and I have been secret whereas you wanted everyone to know and that's why you did not get it?

Don't get me wrong. I wanted to. DAMN, did I want to?

We dated for two weeks before I let you make a big deal.

After that, I gave you what you wanted.

We had sex. Let you tell the story it was deep and passionate.

And I wish I could have agreed but I sadly did not.

Found out later from your brother that you cried for almost 3 weeks after that.

When you found out from a long line of telephone that I was ready to move on.

Imprinted Human pt 1

Hello you.

Although it's not your turn this is where I realized I had to have *You.*

And so far what I wanted I got.

Sadly not this time. You were spoken for and happy.

I may have been evil but not once would I break Girl Code.

Computer Class. Boy was I a kiss ass in this class.

I don't even know how I got anything done.

Every few minutes I'd catch myself daydreaming about you.

You fucking talked to me about everything and it honestly made me start to think I was going crazy.

Days before school was over I was telling everyone I was going to miss them over the break and laughing about the good times.

You said it was cool knowing me and we became friends.

I had to get over this dumb crush.

SO I found him the week before summer.

You were still in my head.

We moved that summer.

All my friends asked what happened to me but you didn't.

Why didn't *you*?

Mathias I. Brookes

Country Boy

Honestly, our time was so short I'm not sure I truly should add you to this.

We were friends the whole school year.

Last two months of school I needed a distraction.

Lucky me you thought summer would be a fun time to go on dates.

So we started before school was over.

We mainly kissed and held hands.

Perfect gentleman

Not

Summer hit; dates happened more and more.

And that's when things became very fast-paced.

The hand holding became you holding my breast the kissing turned into you kissing my body in different places.

We fucked in your truck it was the most unpleasant out of all the times things that had happened in my life.

I went from not wanting to move to wanting it more than anything.

For once I felt used and wasn't the one doing the using.

When we left you said "I don't want to do long distance, but if you come back that would be cool"

You blocked me the next week.

Mathias I. Brookes

College Minded Man

Fuck I don't want to add you to this story

You are the first of many fuck ups I made to defy that woman!

Hell, those women, plural.

New school, New Girl. I'm a mystery to them.

Who wouldn't want to know me?

I held up very well for a while. I had a boyfriend. He was a fucking young saint but sadly you happened.

Older and smart, We had so much in common and Understood me in a way others couldn't.

I didn't like emotions. You told me to end my ties first.

So I did just that.

And Boy was I happy I did!

We did it too many times to count.

Shit too many places at that. If I were to pass them the 1st thing to pop up in my mind would be you.

You were a fucking animal but also very gentle.

Almost made me forget how fucked up I was.

The more we did it the more I realized I kind of need emotions.

Lucky for me you saw it and said you wanted to end things. Because I would have never stopped.

One thing I hate is it took you so long.

You even said "Too bad I'm leaving next year or I'd keep you"

True words of someone who has a problem.

And with that Mister Urkel you kissed me goodbye.

Deadly Dick

I don't want to give you the joy of even being on this list but hell you used me the most!

This is just The Beginning.

We met when I was 15 going on 16 and stayed together 2 and a half years on and off.

I let you use me the most!

I let you get into my head.

You spoiled me in material and emotional ways. We were Best Friends!

I needed you

You learned my drug; and became my supplier.

Fucking two and a half years on and off.

Thank you for being my biggest enabler but also Fuck you!

I was there when you wanted to do many things.

I let you talk me into running away from my duty as a big sister.

You are the biggest reason I have a year tattooed on my body because you used your web of white lies to make me so unsure of myself that I wanted to die.

I ended up in an insane asylum in Florida.

Got to meet Jesus in a black 16-year-old's body!

when it was time for us to break up you posted every nude you ever made me take.

Two years later you came to visit and asked for sex, and like a damaged dumb ass I let you.

No Fucking More

You gave me many scars that my husband is still helping heal!

Best Friends Family

OH Shit!

I can't believe it's your turn!

They said My Best Friend's Brother but I used My Best Friend's cousin!

I was so sick of the same old same old!

Hell, I even made you fight someone to prove how much you wanted me!

You were better than Mister Best Friend!

And I Knew better than to think you'd have learned by now my routine!

I use men and throw them away when I hate them; which was normally very fast.

Since you were a fucking linebacker body you always made me feel like I was the smallest thing ever!

Thank you for always being there!

I played with you on my off with others and that was wrong!

I started and ended things and it wasn't bad but I started to hate that
I had no effect on you because that was also my drug.

The fact that guys seemed to chase me fueled me.

You were able to look at me without wanting sex or anything.

The first and last challenge I learned from you!

Hell, your fucking Brother even wanted me and I was tempted to
do it to piss you off but I couldn't bring myself to do it.

Crazy Fucker

Hello Mister Crazy

My word you Got Me

FUCKED UP!!!!!

We met because your family is friends with mine.

Now you were very kind when I first met you.

I didn't need you for my drug because I had many people wrapped
around my fingers by the time you came along.

That's why you got on my radar!

You kept coming.

And what helped you is that My Mother Fucked up so bad!

AGAIN.

So I wanted to piss her and my aunt off since they wanted so badly for me to do shit anyway!

You were given one chance; you took that and ran with it.

YOU Hurt me, I think you loved seeing my tears though!

Like it fueled you!

And after that, we dated for maybe 3 more weeks.

I was scared to end it, who was going to believe me?

You took it 3 more times.

I was fucking scared to say no!

Until I couldn't fake it anymore.

I had to end things and guess what you did Told my aunt I gave it up so easy and She Fucking believed you!

Why; because your mom said "He would never do anything like that. She pursued him."

Hell even after a few years you found out where i worked and would not leave me the fuck alone!

"You would come in and say maybe we should try again?"

"Give me your number."

One of my customers had to help me out because I froze.

I still hate you for that

Small Intermission

Now a Grown woman, I can say I needed to find myself.

I found this thing called the Internet.

I know it's crazy to think I couldn't use two things a website and an app, you guys were my best friends for the longest.

And can I just say I went through maybe 30 or 40 women and men.

You guys are part of me that will never grow out of.

Helped me to learn things about myself that I will make sure to teach my daughter so she doesn't have to learn from strangers.

You guys helped me learn parts of myself I never knew were there.

I truly feel without this period in my life (I'll call it an intermission).

I shut all my emotions off, I didn't think of them as people but as conquests.

I became a lady in red lipstick not caring who I hurt in my wake.

Thank you but you also made it worse for those that came after I started to show no mercy!

The Mean Girl's Boyfriend

This one is going to ruffle some feathers.

You are a funny one.

For more reasons than one.

For starters, we broke up because it was said I cheated on you with a girl.

Next, you cheated on your girlfriend with me.

You came to me when I was lonely and looking for a friend.

That was a great ruse until it wasn't.

The funny part you were never touchy-feely.

That day it was like you had to be near me.

It started with "Here's what we should do."

Next "No Kissing I might really do something I regret"

Finally it was "We have to do it with you bent over because if I look at you I'll feel bad"

Your rules were dumb but I was only fine with this because it was my leverage for the next time she wanted to be the Mean Girl.

The girl who had no shred of guilt for lying about me.

Who had me questioning parts of me that I hated but also started to think let's use this to my advantage.

In the end it's my own fault but I had no guilt

Imprinted Human pt 2

Hello Again

I told you I always get what I want.

Years later life has put you back in my path.

Sorry for almost any of your girlfriends that year

You cheated many times in that Truck.

You promised me you'd always be there for me no matter what I needed!

And oh did I make you think I needed you so much

The very 1st time I didn't even realize it was happening.

Like most of my fuck up, this one starts with my mom fucking up.

Two days before Christmas

And she decided to fucking start a fight with my stepfather again. I needed to get away.

I'm with my best friend. He falls asleep kinda late, so it's time for me to go home sadly.

"Matti you can't walk, It's night and scary for a tiny person like you." you stated

I wanted to hit you for being so condensing but I thought why not.

You could tell there was something wrong so we stopped
somewhere and talked for what felt like hours.

I will take the blame for the 1st move because I had to know. I
asked why you were being so nice to me.

You answered, "We are great friends and I couldn't bear to see you
sad."

So I asked how far you were willing to go to make me happy?

Before you could answer I kissed you

I never knew how good it would feel to get what you wanted.

You not only kissed back but you gave me passion.

One thing lead to another and well like all others we fucked.

I said we can't do that ever again because it was wrong.

And your words were "No matter what I'll always be there for you
no matter what you need."

The next time we saw each other I fucked up and started a thing I
never knew I needed so much.

You gave me the drug I needed and boy if I wasn't an addict before
I just earned the title!

Trafficker

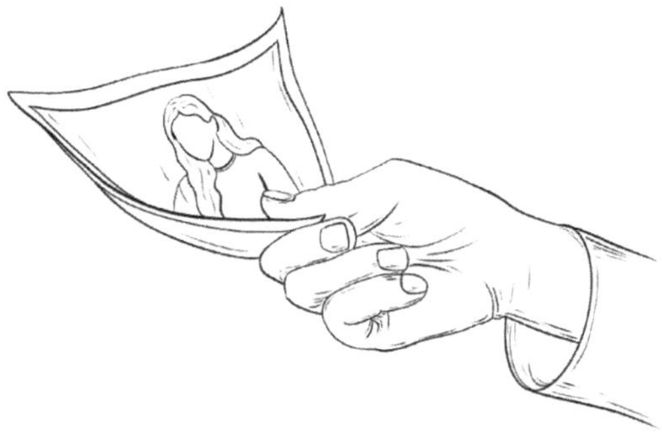

Hello Ass

You were in a whole different city!

I had become engulfed by your words while they were nothing special; I felt like I was on cloud nine.

I would make plans revolving around your involvement.

Dude I even had my friends do trips just to bring you to me.

You made me think it was going to mean us and only us.

Hell, the only thing you honestly had was my drug and I needed it to not feel like a deranged Bitch.

Sex sucked but I didn't for once want to use you because my family had all but made me feel so alone so I thought why the fuck not!

Little did I know you were such a dumb ass!

A Fucking Bitch wanted to kill me because you are "so great"

Thought I was running but I had decided she could have you!

There was nothing to keep You had no job and no plan for your fucking life.

And hunny I thank you for wanting to fight me. I hope your little family is all you guys wanted!

Honestly, If it wasn't for you I wouldn't have been looking for a coping skill, and I wouldn't have found my husband.

So Thank you

Crashed Landing

Dating apps can be such a huge Fucking problem.

I mean you helped me get my way with a lot of things but you also made me so fucking lonely until I met HIM

Honey This book I skipped a lot of steps in fear you would want to read this one day.

I met you and thought great, same old same old.

Fucking Hell was I wrong!

Just from fucking talking you made me rethink life in a matter of fucking minutes.

HELL Seconds

You made me want to think of that middle school love where I plan our lives and draw my name a million times with your last name.

Let's start with the first date. You refused to let me pay!

Then you had errands and convinced me to let go and have fun!

After all, I had been through that past year, I turned into a workaholic.

I took a leap of faith and let go.

Next, You brought me a fucking huge Bear!

Just because I was smiling and you thought "why not?"

I then was like fuck it.

You are now *Mine*

I could not let this happy feeling go after having it for just a few hours.

As time goes by life wanted to tear us the fuck down!

We found out We were expecting !

A baby Girl!

We decided to do it!

And then decided we Are going to kick Life's Ass this time around!

Then we found out more shit along the way and life thought it was going to ruin us.

But not this time or any.

Thank you hun for coming into contact with this body and deciding to stay!

Not the End

People of Earth

I'm not here to say that every man in my life is to blame,

But some of them are!

Some of them deserve to rot in jail but I'm not going to do that. I have forgiven them but I will never forget them!

There are some people who have been abused as i have been but please listen.

There are really bad fucking people in this world but there are also good people!

Let's not cut down the good and let the bad get away!

I wrote this and told a few of my stories hoping to get to the fucking point.

I to this day hate most men because it's in most cases them who use the power and run with it!

I also hate women Because some of us make excuses for those same men!

America has made young woman think that we have to be perfect at all times; whereas men can fuck up many times and still they are perfect!

In my life time I've fucked up a lot and been tossed to the side; yet someone i know has fucked up more to the point children were in danger and yet he's been almost rewared.

Last thing i will say My door is always open to any and every one will I trust you no, Will i give you a chance yes.